it's
not
too
late

it's not too late

a framework for restoring
a troubled marriage

DR. MIKE DUFFY

ISBN 979-8-9894314-3-4

All Scripture is taken from the AUTHORIZED KING JAMES VERSION.

Edited by Melanie Engle, Eagle Eye Editing
Cover design and typesetting by Jenneth Dyck

Table of Contents

Introduction

way. So, consider this when your dream marriage becomes a nightmare: it is time to get help. Where will you begin? "*Ointment and perfume rejoice the heart: so doth the sweetness of a man's friend by hearty counsel* (Proverbs 27:9)." It is the "hearty counsel" I want to provide for you as you consider your situation today.

Hope for daily living:

We should learn from the past and look toward the future, as we live today. The past cannot be re-lived, but it can be leveraged.

A troubled marriage usually contains some difficult or unpleasant baggage from the past. This can be a major barrier to successful restoration if it is not properly addressed. Although we cannot change the past, we can learn from it. And although we can learn from it, we must be careful not to choose to live in the past. We should learn from the past and look toward the future, as we live today. That seems to be a healthy formula for living.

We should never lose sight of the fact that a marriage between two people is a marriage between two sinners. Even though they may have been reconciled to God, they still have to deal with the influence of both a sinful nature and powerful flesh. They also live in a world that has contrary thoughts and opinions to what the Creator has established. And so, failures and disappointments are possible all along the journey.

For example, my own knowledge base today is made up of some principled instruction that I have learned from the Bible in my adult years and is coupled with some good examples from a few people that have touched my life over these past decades. I had little instruction and no training about marriage before my wife and I married over fifty-five years ago. I have come to understand that many others were as ill-prepared for marriage as Geri and I were.

The examples I had for what a marriage should be like were not good examples. My parents' contribution was that of a shattered marriage and a tragic divorce while I was in junior high school. My observations of the world in which I lived, which often resembled a war zone where the institution of marriage was under constant barrage by the enemies of God, were not good either. I have probably learned more about "what not to do" than "what to do" from those observations. Failure, whether watching it or experiencing it, can be a good instructor.

> *One thing that has been quite helpful to me in studying the marriage relationship is realizing the Bible addresses the relative issues through two lenses.*
> - *The first lens is God's original intent. We see his intent for marriage clearly in Genesis 2.*
> - *The second lens sees a fallen world. Sin changed everything! Although failing in the area of original intent, God has not left us hopeless. He has provided a way forward through redemption, reconciliation, and restoration.*

While it would be easy to blame others and seek solace by casting aspersions on them, I would be foolish not to admit that my own mistakes and failures have been numerous, and that they are the source of some of the difficulties my wife and I have had to face along our journey together. I have no doubt that there have been times that I have been my own worst enemy.

However, what I have learned from the Scriptures over these past decades (through both diligent study and many counseling sessions trying to help those struggling in their marriages) has taught me a lot of what God intends marriage to be. His teaching and training are quite thorough and highly reliable. After all, He is the designer and creator of marriage. And so, with little reliance on my own expertise or experience, I share with you some of these wonderful truths God has taught me.

Another great challenge most face in their marriage is one of expectation or confidence. We may think, "I cannot change," or, "My spouse will never change." These are common feelings. But, if we have hope of restoring a faltering marriage, that hope is the encouragement one needs so that they can put forth their best effort. Remember, though: our hope needs to be put in the right place. Our real hope is in the Lord. He can help us both change and heal. His mercy, demonstrated in forgiveness, His enabling grace in restoration and change, and his unchangeable Word for counsel and guidance are enough. They can get the job done effectively!

With that predicate established, the following is a framework of biblical truth to work through to begin the process of restoring a marriage to God's original intent for it. Whether you go through this alone or with your spouse, you can connect the dots of your own life experience by using this book to guide your thinking and mediation. While this is not intended to be theologically exhaustive, it does provide key foundational Bible principles from which you can begin your journey. As you seek God and His will for your life through His Word, He will show you a clear pathway to restoring what He intended to be beautiful for you. Your role is to seek, learn, and apply the Truth in a spirit of submission to God's authority. Once you take the first step by faith, God will see the sincerity of your heart, and He will be with you throughout your journey.

Chapter One

Refreshing Our Understanding

A good place to begin is remembering what God intended your marriage to be. We can begin this process by reading Genesis 1 and 2 (there is a full text in the Appendix). May I suggest that you read these two chapters from the Bible slowly and thoughtfully? Try to put yourself in the grandstand, watching the Creator do his work, and carefully consider each thing that he does. Each piece of God's elaborate puzzle, when put in its proper place, helps you see the big picture of what God was doing. You may benefit from reading it through more than once. Take your time to read and meditate on what you are reading.

In these two chapters you will be reminded of the following points.

God Made Man

Man is created in the image of God, that is, in construct, image, likeness, and resemblance (Genesis 1:26-28). God made mankind unique, above all other life that He created.

Man has a moral component. The first man was created righteous and innocent in a dispensation before sin existed in the world. He knew what was right, and he did what was right. He exercised his free will in a way that pleased God every time. And, therefore, he was innocent. Not a trace of guilt because of sin. This helps us understand what God's original plan for mankind was.

Man has a material element, the **body**, which can be considered his temporal housing. His body was formed from dust of the ground (Genesis 2:7) and will return after physical death to dust (Genesis 3:19). For now, however, it is the vessel that serves as home to man's soul and spirit. I have always been amazed at the immense scope of God's creative genius and His wonderful imagination in that no two people are alike. Each of us is unique; body, soul, and spirit. King David expressed this same amazement like this: "*I will praise thee; for I am fearfully and wonderfully made: marvellous are thy works; and that my soul knoweth right well* (Psalm 139:14)." David acknowledged God's creative work, and that he was part of it. That is where you should begin.

The man also has an immaterial element, his **soul** (Genesis 2:7). The soul is everlasting. His soul is made up of his intellect, emotions, and will. Mentally, he was rational and volitional, meaning he could reason and make choices. His intellect and emotions would inform his free will as he faced the issues of life; then, with his will, he would make decisions, just like we do today.

The soul is often referred to in Scripture as the "heart of the man." King Solomon taught his son this wonderful truth about the relationship between the heart and the will: "*Keep thy heart with all diligence; for out of it are the issues of life* (Proverbs 4:23)."

In my opinion, this is one of the most critical issues of the Christian life. Solomon was telling his son to be diligent about "guarding" or protecting his heart from wrong influences, because when an issue of life came along, the condition of his heart would impact his choices. If his heart was "godly" when facing the issue, he would make a godly response. However, if his heart was carnal or ungodly, his choices would also be carnal or ungodly.

And so, it is the same for you. As you begin this journey, you will want a heart that is free from wrong influences and is surrendered to the will of God, so you can think clearly and make the best choices.

Man has a **spirit** so that he can relate to and fellowship with God, Who is spirit (John 4:24). This is man's most important relationship. Knowing God in this personal way is the essence of eternal life (John 17:3). Man was created as a social being, and so, he was capable of having fellowship and participating in a relationship with the Creator.

Remember, it was the unrighteousness of our sin that had separated us from God. God's primary reason for sending His only begotten Son to the cross was to save us from our sin, bringing us back into fellowship with Him. Personal relationship with you is what He is most interested in!

Man was created. He did not evolve from some lower form of life. The history of mankind from generation to generation is recorded in the Bible. Your ancestors are people, not monkeys, tadpoles, or some abstract residue from an explosion. You are designed by the Creator for a purpose He has determined.

"***Male & female*** *created He them* (Genesis 1:27)." God determined each person's gender to fulfill His purpose in their life, in their marriage, and in their family. In a marriage, the man is the husband (a male person), and the woman is the wife (a female person). The eternal Word of God is settled on this issue, and so, too, do we need to be settled.

God determined each person's gender to fulfill His purpose in their life, in their marriage, and in their family. "Be what He determined for you!" He expects nothing else!

A special note of caution here: popular culture has greatly attacked this truth in recent years. Be careful not to believe the lies they have propagated. The destruction of the family is a primary goal of the enemies of God, and that is the source of the confusion in the culture.

Mankind is created for **God's purpose and pleasure**, not our own purpose and pleasure (Revelation 4:11). This is important to understand. God has a "will" for your life. You are part of His big plan! If you spend time pursuing God's will, you will not have to imagine or create a will or plan of your own. God's stated purpose for mankind was to be fruitful and multiply, replenishing the earth, and to have dominion over the animal kingdom—subduing the earth and bringing it into subjection. It clearly states this in these chapters.

Adam's first responsibilities included dressing and keeping the garden of Eden. Work was an avenue for fulfillment and provision as he obeyed God. He was to be a protector or watchman of sorts, both the gardener and the guard. In choosing to fulfill his responsibility, he would glorify God.

"It Is Not Good That Man Should Be Alone"

God's declaration was that it was "not becoming," or "appropriate," that man should be alone, or by himself. This statement made by God is recorded in Genesis 2:18, and it is such a significant statement. It seems to be the original basis for God establishing marriage. We can see this in God's response to this truth: *"I will make him an help meet for him"*—a helper to fulfill the man's God-given purpose. I think we must start our understanding of the entire concept of marriage with this foundational statement. In doing so, it adds much clarity to the issues we face in marriage. Man was incomplete for the purpose, and God knew it!

The foundational principle of marriage: "It is not good that man should be alone.

– Genesis 2:18

So, God made the first woman and presented her to Adam (Genesis 2:21-22). Adam called her "woman" because she was taken out of man (Genesis 2:23). This was the first marriage union. It would be an exclusive relationship based on unity. She came out of the man and was for the man.

This union would be unique in its transparency—each one having an intimate knowledge of the other's very being, including their body, soul, and spirit—and it would be built around trust and devotion. The marriage would be preserved by their discretion as they shared their intimacy with no other than their partner. Their relationship was private. It would be a relationship that would include sacrifice, surrender, and submission as the couple journeyed together.

The woman (a female), the wife, was to be a "help meet," or helper. She was created for the man. She would "complete" him so that he, with her help, could fulfill God's will. This was not simply a marriage of convenience where two people would dwell under the same roof while doing their own thing! It was God's intention to put them together. Do not miss the importance and value of this foundational truth!

"Therefore," the Action Plan

Because of all that is mentioned previously, man was to leave his father and mother. He would no longer be under their authority (Genesis 2:24). He will understand and pursue the will of God for his own life, not fulfill mom and dad's dream for his life. That is not to say their guidance and input is not important; it is. This teaches us that the goal for parents is to raise the children, whom God has entrusted to their care, to know God and to love Him. In doing so, the parents are preparing the child to seek God's will and do it. God can and will reveal his plan for those children to those children at the time of God's choosing. Parents must caution themselves against developing aspirations for their kids that are in conflict with what God has in store for them. Losing sight of this truth has put a lot of families on a destructive trajectory. Parents need to teach and train their children in the

We could all benefit from heeding the quote by F. E. Marsh more than a century ago:

The will of God – Nothing more, Nothing less, and Nothing else.

things of God, and to help the kids recognize and develop the gifts and talents that God has given them.

Thus, God created marriage between a man and woman, establishing the first institution on Earth: the "family." We sometimes say that God created the home, and, in our thinking, we mean family. But let me suggest that we should distinguish the difference between "family" (clan, circle of relatives) and the home or "household" (a dwelling place). The marriage is a sacred relationship, not a place or household. Remembering this truth is critical to your journey.

Man is the leader of the family, the head. There is a sense that headship is like an executive position. He is the leader of the family to understand and execute the will of God.

Woman is the completer of the man—the leader, head, or guide—of the household (I Timothy 5:14). This leadership could be likened to a management position. She manages the affairs of the family as they relate to the household where the family resides. It is very important for the protector and provider to have this help. As she carries this burden, their family moves forward in God's will. His role is crucial, and so is hers. That is what God intended!

The man cleaves unto his wife, meaning to cling to or keep close. He is a one-woman man indicating this is an exclusive relationship, grounded in integrity. It is to be an intimate relationship. The intimacy should be present in the body, soul, and spirit of both members of the union.

> A healthy marriage is characterized by unity (oneness), and is gained through intimacy, preserved with discretion.

Together, they "shall be one flesh" (i.e., kindred; blood relations). This is the weaving together of a relationship (Ephesians 5:31). The one-flesh relationship is characterized by unity (oneness), and is gained through intimacy, preserved with discretion, and impacts all three parts of man.

In the body there is physical intimacy. We understand that sexual activity is part of developing physical intimacy. The marriage relationship is deepened by this function. The unique secrets and pleasures of physical intimacy strengthen the union. It is to be pleasurable for both, and there should be a fervent desire to please the other partner. You may want to look at the Song of Solomon to help develop a greater understanding of physical intimacy. There you will see expressions of love such as kisses (1:2), embraces (2:6), eye contact ("the eyes of doves"), meaning eyes of love focused exclusively on their lover, and the God-given appetite for passion and love, which, if not satisfied, can become a big problem in the marriage.

Physical intimacy is also a component of fulfilling God's purpose of being fruitful and multiplying. "*Lo, children are an heritage of the LORD: and the fruit of the womb is his reward* (Psalm 127:3)." We understand from several Old Testament examples that it is God who opens and closes the womb. Not every couple will have children, but it should be clearly understood that having them is determined by God.

In the soul, their intimacy is intellectual and emotional. This provides unity both in the philosophy of life and the worldview they hold. They share their most private and secretive thoughts with each other. Thus, the trust developed in this union becomes greater and greater as time goes by. They share their emotions with each other and draw comfort from one another to ease or soothe these feelings, and in doing so, strengthen their bond. They put principles before feelings, but do not leave the feelings out! They are soulmates in the sense of knowing about, empathizing with, and deferring to each other within the bonds of their marriage for the duration of their lifetime. Once again, this is preserved by the boundaries of discretion.

The spiritual intimacy keeps them strong in their relationship with God as they pray together and honor their commitment to each other to follow God's leading in their lives and perform their God-given roles in the family. Encouraging each other in their personal walk with the Lord brings strength to their marriage. They pick each other up in the times of weakness

Two are better than one; because they have a good reward for their labour. For if they fall, the one will lift up his fellow: but woe to him that is alone when he falleth; for he hath not another to help him up.
— Ecclesiastes 4:9-10

and failure. As they fulfill God's purpose and live godly as husband and wife, they glorify God.

Simply "knowing" these truths does not produce the right outcome: "doing" does, by the grace of God! As much as you might think this is so "idealistic" and far from reality, it is all possible in Christ. It is part of His plan for our abundant life! Trusting Him is your challenge. Just rehearse in your mind for a moment the lyrics of this song we teach our children from their earliest ability to comprehend:

When we walk with the Lord in the light of His Word,
What a glory He sheds on our way!
While we do His good will, He abides with us still,
And with all who will trust and obey

Trust and obey, for there's no other way
To be happy in Jesus, but to trust and obey!

Sounds so simple, doesn't it? Well, it is not complicated to understand. The difficulty is in making the choice: God's will or my will. As a friend of mine used to say quite frequently: "There are just two choices on the shelf, pleasing God or pleasing self." We must make the right choices every day.

"There are just two choices on the shelf,
pleasing God or pleasing self."
— Ken Collier, The Wilds Christian Camp

Questions to Consider

Who have you been trying to please?

_____

_____

How has that been working out for you?

_____

_____

Are there any areas of this section in which your understanding is in conflict?

_____

_____

Has any portion of this section revealed your unhappiness or rebellion about who you are?

_____

_____

Has any portion of this section caused you to admit that you have been listening to the wrong voices and you know it has influenced your thinking in a negative way?

_____

_____

Are there things in your life or relationship you have thought could not change?

_____

_____

How strong has your relationship with the Lord been throughout your difficult times?

_____

_____

Who, or what, has been discouraging you in your marriage? Why?

_____

_____

How discrete are you in your relationships? (You may have been undermining yourself!)

_____

_____

Chapter Two

Reframing the Issue

D id you start wrong or go wrong? Having been reminded of God's intention for marriage, do your best to answer this question; it will help you frame the issues you are facing. It is an important step in this journey.

Take a few moments here to write out your answer. To help your focus, try to limit your response to three sentences.

_____

_____

_____

_____

_____

_____

_____

_____

_____

_____

_____

_____

Why Did You Marry?

Fixing a problem is difficult if you cannot name the problem. Do you remember why you wanted to get married? Making an honest personal assessment here will help you move forward in your life. Try writing out a brief, although thoughtful, answer to each of these questions:

- Was it the will of God for you to be married, or was it something else?

  _____

  _____

  _____

  _____

- Did you have an agenda that was different than God's agenda?

  _____

  _____

  _____

  _____

- What is on your agenda now? (If your agenda is not in line with God's agenda, then do not change partners; change your agenda!)

  _____

  _____

  _____

  _____

- Recognize that you may be your own worst enemy—it is true that the world, the flesh, and the devil will seek to draw you away from God's will, but you have a will too! Exercise it in surrender and submission to the will of God. This is a choice that you, and only you, can make, by the grace of God (1 Corinthians 10:13 and James 1:12-20).

How Prepared Were You for Marriage?

I imagine there is a huge gap between desire and preparedness as most marriages begin. We all want that perfect marriage. However, our preparation to make that happen is usually grossly lacking. Ignorance and expedience often drive us toward the big day!

How much instruction did you receive to prepare for marriage? What were the sources of the instruction for both the teacher and the curriculum? Was the instruction secular, from the common culture, or was it biblical? Let me encourage you to write a paragraph or two about the instruction you received and where it came from. Then, write out the thoughts you have today of the outcome of that instruction. What does your honest evaluation today tell you about the adequacy or appropriateness of that instruction?

What instruction did I receive?

_____

_____

_____

_____

_____

_____

What are the examples you saw? I would encourage you to write out a list of examples you had in your life that made an impression on your mind. Then, write a few sentences to describe the impressions made from each of those examples. They might be good examples or bad examples; you can learn from both. From some examples we learn what to do, and others we learn what not to do.

Examples I had, and what I learned from them.

_____

_____

_____

_____

What Is Your Desire Going Forward?

What is your honest goal? What do you truly want to do going forward in your life? Do not write out what you think will happen. This is not the time to make a prediction. You are simply stating what is truly in your heart to do. Stop right here and write out the answer!

In my heart, I want...

_____

_____

_____

_____

Questions to Consider

Who was your greatest influence when you were considering getting married? Why?

_____

_____

_____

What do you consider the two biggest mistakes you have made regarding marriage?

_____

_____

_____

What would you have done differently to prepare for marriage?

_____

_____

_____

If you started well, where do you think your relationship began to take a bad turn?

_____

_____

_____

Chapter Three

Roles in a Marriage

What is your role in the marriage? I recommend you read Ephesians 4 and 5 as we consider this issue (full text in Appendix). These two chapters are so informative as to the vastness of the plan God has for your life. Grasping the truths contained therein provides a treasure trove of knowledge and wisdom that will help you embrace your God-given roles and responsibilities. Your marriage will require personal discipline and determination, and so understanding these chapters will help you greatly. Colossians 3 and 4 (full text in Appendix) are complimentary to Ephesians 4 and 5 and will provide you with additional help and encouragement. Spend as much time as needed to master these passages. I would suggest reading them through several times in a short period of time.

An Agreement to Fulfill My God Given Role (Vows)

One of the most significant issues and elements when entering a marriage is the agreement together to fulfill God-given roles and responsibilities. This is typically formalized in a wedding ceremony through wedding vows. The apostle Paul gives some wise counsel about this in Ephesians chapter five.

[17] Wherefore be ye not unwise, but understanding what the will of the Lord is. [18] And be not drunk with wine, wherein is excess; but be filled with the Spirit; [19] Speaking to yourselves in psalms and hymns and spiritual songs, singing and making melody in your heart to the Lord; [20] Giving thanks always for all things unto God and the Father in the name of our Lord Jesus Christ; [21] Submitting yourselves one to another in the fear of God.

Submitting yourselves one to another in the fear of God.

In preparation for making this commitment, the apostle Paul says to be filled with the Spirit (verse 18). That pretty much means full of the Spirit of God and empty of self. He contrasts the filling of the Spirit with being drunk with wine. In other words, no outside influence is controlling your life or diminishing your resolve to love and serve God. Your free will is operating freely! This means to be right with God through personal examination, personal walk, and personal discipline, which could be considered the continual emptying of self and selfishness. We do not want the Holy Spirit to be grieved or quenched by our sinful behavior.

Being filled with the Spirit demonstrates a desire to serve God that says, "I want to do the will of God so my life on earth glorifies Him!" Andrew Murray authored a book expressing this desire titled *Absolute Surrender.* One review of the book made this statement, "*Andrew Murray's splendid treatise guides Christians to a greater, more mature, and blissfully profound relationship with the Lord.*" This is what Paul is encouraging the couple to do. He exhorts them to make these commitments with God as their witness.

Singing and making melody in your heart to the Lord is the result of being at peace with God (verse 19). It is evidenced by joy, the praise of God, and rejoicing at the work of God in your life, which will, in turn, produce the giving of thanks unto the Lord always for all things or manifesting a spirit of gratitude (verse 20).

> *Genuine submission to God and His leadership in your life is evidenced by joy, the praise of God, and rejoicing at the work of God producing the giving of thanks unto the Lord.*

Being grateful and having the peace of God prepares the way and enables the next act of the will: submitting yourselves one to another. Think carefully through this thought: together, each is committing to the other to fulfill their role in a godly manner. This is perhaps the most important issue, and the most difficult to commit to and to fulfill. The selfish nature of man is in constant conflict with this step in God's process. However, exercising obedience as you live together as a family, with God's glory in view, is the discipline you need for a happy, fruitful marriage. It will likely be the difference between enjoying your marriage or enduring it.

Wives, Submit Yourself to Your Own Husband

Ephesians 5:22-24 is instruction to the wife to submit to her own husband. Well, this is not a very popular position in modern day American culture! Both she and her husband need a clear understanding of what this passage is teaching. It reads as follows.

> [22] Wives, submit yourselves unto your own husbands, as unto the Lord. [23] For the husband is the head of the wife, even as Christ is the head of the church: and he is the saviour of the body. [24] Therefore as the church is subject unto Christ, so let the wives be to their own husbands in every thing.

Her submission to her husband is as though she were submitting unto the person of the Lord Jesus Christ Himself (verse 22). It should be her desire to enter marriage with the intention of completing the

It should be her desire to enter marriage with the intention of completing the husband. husband. She understands this is her role, and she desires to fulfill it in the marriage relationship in the spirit of, "I want to do the will of God so that my life on earth glorifies Him!"

When tempted to rebel or reject her husband's leadership, she should consider what she would do if it was Jesus Himself who was the one she would rebel against or reject. That would likely expose the spirit of her submission.

She understands that the husband is the head of the wife, making him the head of the family (verse 23). He is the leader who bears the responsibility for the family and is accountable to God for it. This is of primary significance to understand. God is able to—and will—hold the husband accountable. She has no intention or desire to undermine or supplant his leadership. She will need to resist the temptation to do so in times of weakness and failure by her husband. This is certainly a "keeping the heart with all diligence" issue! She wants his leadership for her life, too. She looks to her husband for it, and she lets him do it. Her selfish nature will constantly hurl moments of temptation her way! By God's grace she rejects and escapes those temptations.

She is to submit "in everything" (verse 24). She is to let her husband lead, and she is to support his leadership. She should not seek to manipulate him, as that would undermine this principle. That would be feigned, or hypocritical submission, and it would not fool God. She can voice her interests or concerns, but then she should submit to his leadership. Healthy communication about issues and input from the wife is good, but the decision burden is his role. This would include establishing goals and setting priorities in the family.

In Paul's summary and application, he points out that the wife is to reverence her husband (Ephesians 5:33). This means to venerate or respect him, and to treat him with deference or reverential obedience. Although this may be difficult sometimes because of the man's failures, behavior, or personality, she must reverence him because of his position in God's order. This is how she glorifies God.

Husbands, Love Your Wives

Next, Paul shifts his focus to the husband in Ephesians 5:25-31. It reads as follows.

> [25] Husbands, love your wives, even as Christ also loved the church, and gave himself for it; [26] That he might sanctify and cleanse it with the washing of water by the word, [27] That he might present it to himself a glorious church, not having spot, or wrinkle, or any such thing; but that it should be holy and without blemish. [28] So ought men to love their wives as their own bodies. He that loveth his wife loveth himself. [29] For no man ever yet hated his own flesh; but nourisheth and cherisheth it, even as the Lord the church: [30] For we are members of his body, of his flesh, and of his bones. [31] For this cause shall a man leave his father and mother, and shall be joined unto his wife, and they two shall be one flesh.

The husband is to love the wife in the same manner that Christ loved the church. He gave himself for it! Imagine this husband—we have a perfect example of what our leadership should look like! It is Jesus Christ. Jesus sacrificed His life for her benefit.

And so, the husband is to love his wife by sacrificing himself for her benefit. That includes providing for her and protecting her as she submissively guides the home and nurtures the family.

A husband loves his wife spiritually by being interested in and concerned for her personal relationship with the Lord. He nourishes her soul intellectually and emotionally, validating her role and addressing things that are of concern to her.

Peter exhorts husbands to this also: "*Likewise, ye husbands, dwell with them according to knowledge, giving honour unto the wife, as unto the weaker vessel, and as being heirs together of the grace of life; that your prayers be not hindered* (1 Peter 3:7)." That little phrase "according to knowledge" speaks directly to the intimacy issue. A husband is to intentionally develop a deep understanding of his wife so he can meet her needs. He loves her physically by addressing the needs for her physical health and meeting her intimate needs. He cherishes her by praying for her and outwardly demonstrating his love for her.

In his letter to the church at Colosse, Paul added an interesting requirement for husbands. He said: "*Husbands, love your wives, and be not bitter against them* (Colossians 3:19)." They are not to become angry with or be embittered toward their wives. "Why might this happen?" one might ask. Good question!

The marriage relationship is going to experience some transitions that carry the potential to create some of these feelings. When the "honeymoon" is over and the couple is settling into their routine of life, they might experience change because their understanding of each other has been greatly increased. It may be that the "mystery" has subsided, and fantasy has turned to reality.

This should help us understand the significance of getting to know someone well before committing oneself to them. This can be a tough lesson to learn by experience. If that is what has happened to you, do not melt away in despair and discouragement; learn from it so you can teach others who have not yet made the mistake of hastily made decisions about marriage. Then, pick up the lemons and make some lemonade.

Another significant transition that influences relationships is the addition of children. Once they arrive, suddenly the demand for attention changes the level of focus the couple gives to each other. The "sweetie pie" of love and affection is now cut into three pieces instead of two!

The man must keep in mind that she, as his completer, is a gift from God, and offers another point of view on most issues, and that is a woman's point of view.

Another place where a bitter spirit could develop is in the context of a man leading his family. He could easily interpret advice or input from his wife as criticism or a challenge. The man must keep in mind that she, as his completer, is a gift from God, and offers another point of view on most issues, and that is a woman's point of view. Having multiple perspectives to consider in leadership is a blessing, not a curse. As men, we should want to see all the options before we decide. Her thoughts and opinions should be valued. Our sinful pride sometimes puts us in a defensive posture, not willing to take any advice. Our patience may also be put to the test in situations like this.

The antidote for bitterness is good communication, grace, and deference. Use it as often as needed. It will be needed again, and again, and again!

Children, Obey and Honor Your Parents

In both Ephesians 6 and Deuteronomy 6 there is extensive instruction regarding the parents' responsibility with the children God blesses them with. While there is much to study and say about the parent-child relationship, we will limit our comments here to the impact of children on the spousal relationship.

It is a commonly recognized problem that when children arrive on the scene, the husband/wife relationship is challenged. The demand for attention and focus on the children challenges the intimacy of the marriage relationship. Far too often, that challenge causes the couple to begin growing apart as one or both parents focus primarily on the children and may unintentionally neglect the other.

The lack of agreement with the philosophy of raising children can also become a source of great contention. The diminished agreement and lack of focus can become quite unhealthy! The Bible is quite sufficient to address these disagreements. Do not leave God out of the discussion.

Both the husband and wife should make it a priority to maintain and strengthen their relationship with each other. They can succeed at this by first understanding and acknowledging the potential threat that focusing exclusively on kids brings, and then intentionally acting to prevent this from happening. Letting the demands of the children control the spousal relationship is not good. Denial of this truth will not serve the couple or their children well. Finding time to spend together alone and communicating with each other regularly should be high on the priority list.

The second big issue is this: understanding they are parents before being friends. They have a primary responsibility of teaching and training the children that have been given to them by God. This will include both education and discipline. Being a child's BFF is not the goal!

However, their love for their children fosters an "anything for the children" mentality and all of the parent's desire is toward their children. They begin to form dreams and aspirations of their own for their children and then allow inattention to their spousal relationship to shatter the dreams they once had for each other. This happens by choice and, as such, it means you can make a different choice.

God entrusted the upbringing of the children to the parents. Keep in mind that at some point in time however, the kids are to follow God's leading by leaving their father and mother as they establish a new family. So, we know in advance that raising children takes place only for a season; in contrast, the marriage relationship

> *Keep in mind that at some point in time however, the kids are to follow God's leading by leaving their father and mother as they establish a new family.*

is for a lifetime. Never lose sight of this truth! It is quite common that when the last child leaves the nest, the husband and wife find themselves living with complete strangers! Do not let this happen to you!

The kids are in the process of "becoming." Becoming what? Good question, is it not? The role you have as parents is to bring them up in the nurture and admonition of the Lord. Your focus should be on introducing your children to the Lord so they learn to trust in Him, and so they begin to understand what God's will is for their life.

Recognizing the works of God in your family and acknowledging them to your children is a critical priority in this process. If children do not see the "works of God," God will be no more real to them than the fictitious characters of Santa Claus and the Easter Bunny. They never really see those characters either. When children adopt a fictitious god, there will eventually be parents who have a broken heart and a sense of failure.

Your desires and dreams for your children should be that they, first, know God and, secondly, to do His will. That they understand who God is, that they are saved, and that they are walking with God are your primary teaching and training roles. I cannot overemphasize the importance of teaching them both the Bible and how to study the Bible so this can be a reality in their life. That's it! Leave the "what" and "when" of their future to God. As you begin to identify God's gifting in their lives, help them develop that gifting. Pay attention to what they are interested in. Remember, it is God who puts desires on our hearts, and He will do this with your children, too.

So, as a parent, you should teach your children God's Word. Encourage them to obey God. One early lesson a child must be taught is this: "You cannot have your own way." That means teaching them the dreaded "NO" word.

You will also need to teach them to wait. The more often they get their own way, the more they will desire to have their own way! Well, at what point, then, do you expect them to stop wanting their own way and surrender to God's way? The sooner the better! Too much leniency in this area and you will see the cuteness of infant behavior turn into an all-out rebellion and quest for power in them as a toddler. Do not forget that your children have a will of their own. And remember, they also have a sinful nature!

And since children are to honor and obey their parents, the parents need to provide the structure and discipline to make this happen. Honoring means "to consider precious." The parents need to set a good example so this happens. Consistent instruction and loving discipline are the keys to them setting an example. The Bible teaches us in Hebrews 12:11 that proper discipline yields "the peaceable fruit of righteousness." Do you see the value proposition a child might learn? Controlled behavior leads to favorable outcomes!

> Controlled behavior leads to favorable outcomes!

Parents should be teaming up to ensure this is happening in the home. A disobedient and undisciplined parent will frustrate and discourage the child from honoring or obeying. You see this regularly, particularly at the grocery store or shopping mall.

Questions to Consider

Are there any areas of this section in which your understanding is in conflict with God's Word?

_____

_____

_____

Has any portion of this section revealed your unhappiness or rebellion about who you are?

_____

_____

_____

Has any portion of this section caused you to admit that you have been listening to the wrong voices that have influenced your thinking in a negative way?

_____

_____

_____

Are you seeing some positive action steps you can begin taking immediately?

_____

_____

_____

Chapter 4

Responsibilities in the Family

What are the primary responsibilities of each person in the family? Remembering what God has determined them to be will benefit you on this journey. Oftentimes we let the expectations of others and the pressures of the culture in which we live shape our thinking on these matters. It is important to know what the Creator intended.

The Husband/Father

Equipped and gifted by God, the husband is the head of the family and should lead them in all areas of family life.

As the family provider, he is to consider provision in the areas of shelter, income or increase that meets the family needs, and spiritual leadership. This would include discerning needs, establishing priorities, and making and executing plans to meet them.

He is also to be the protector of the family. Within this responsibility, he should consider the physical, mental, emotional, and spiritual well-being of his family. This is a big task. He should establish the structure and set boundaries that will provide the protection. Then he should exercise himself in this context to make these things a reality for his family.

One area of potential conflict is the area of standards, both personal and family.

He should establish these standards based on principle and teach them to the family. Explaining what the standard is provides the boundary. Explaining why you have the standard adds understanding, which is important to the growth process of the children. Knowing the "why" often helps one do the "what."

I have taught often on the issue of standards and have found it helpful to define a few key words. These words are **principles**, **convictions**, and **standards**.

- *Principles*
- *Convictions*
- *Standards*

The word **principle** is defined as "a fundamental or basic truth." God's truth never changes! "*For ever, O LORD, thy word is settled in heaven* (Psalm 119:89)." That is why we establish the structure and standards with Bible principles. We use Scriptures, and their authority, to establish the standard, and then we teach the principle to give understanding to the persons we are teaching.

The word **"conviction"** is defined as "a state of being convinced of error (negative) or compelled to admit the truth (positive)." This is such an important word in parenting. We want our children to believe and obey by conviction, not just "because I said so!" We want our children to be convinced of truth by the Holy Spirit of God so that they develop a desire to please God and not violate the principles He established. It protects them as well as helps them to grow spiritually.

And the third word is **standard**, which is defined as "a structure built for, or serving as, a base or support." Standards are established to support our convictions and keep us from violating the principles of God. Standards, or rules, are not established in order to gain favor with God, they are meant to protect us from sinning against God and bringing judgment upon our lives. When one understands this, standards then have the positive connotation of being a help and support, rather than projecting the negative connotation of restriction and forbidding, which fosters rebellion.

The husband also has the responsibility to teach and train the children. Ephesians 6:4 says he is to bring them up to maturity in the nurture and admonition of the Lord. To nurture means tutorage, i.e., education or training. By implication, the training means disciplinary correction, including chastening and instruction. Admonition is the "calling attention to" a behavior by providing a mild rebuke or verbal warning, and this is to be done using the ways of God as the standard.

When a father fails at this responsibility, the outcome is provocation of the children to wrath. It creates anger and rebellion in their hearts which is often acted out in the relationships at home.

This can be a source of much confusion for parents. As young men are growing up to become providers and protectors, they develop a sense of independence and a strong will that may serve them well as a leader. A parent must exercise patience and discernment in determining the difference between growth and rebellion, and then acting appropriately to each.

Raising children is a big task. Although Ephesian 6:4 addresses the husband, it should not be overlooked that the wife's role is that of a completer. Together the parents should train and teach their children with a consistent and coordinated effort, not in conflict with each other.

> A parent must exercise patience and discernment in determining the difference between growth and rebellion, and then acting appropriately to each.

Deuteronomy 6 offers much instruction and exhortation to parents for raising children. This passage makes it clear that they are to impart truth to this next generation, making God's Word an ever-present influence in their lives. This is God's generational plan for mankind.

The Wife/Mother

She is equipped and gifted by God to complete the man (Genesis 2:18). She may bear children (Genesis 3:16 and I Timothy 5:14), making her a mother. It is her role to guide the house (I Timothy 5:14). This word "guide" means to be master (or head) of a house—to rule a household and manage family affairs. This does not mean that she supplants the husband's role of being the head, or leader, of the family. As we have pointed out previously, there is a distinction between "family" (clan, circle of relatives) and the home or "household" (a dwelling place).

> She helps protect the family's name and testimony, bringing glory to God.

In Paul's writing to Titus (Titus 2:5), we see that she is to be a "keeper at home." She is to be domestically inclined, a good housekeeper. In fulfilling her role, she helps protect the family's name and testimony, bringing glory to God. As Solomon said, "*A good name is rather to be chosen than great riches, and loving favour rather than silver and gold* (Proverbs 22:1)."

When I consider the roles of the husband and wife, it seems that in the adherence to these roles, man finds great fulfillment in his work as the provider/protector. In the same fashion, the woman finds great fulfillment and value in managing the family affairs and keeping order in the home. The peaceful harmony of these two, as they fulfill their purpose together, brings glory to God.

The Children

The parent's role is teaching and training, and so we can say the child's role is learning and applying the ways of God. Solomon taught his son to "*Train up a child in the way he should go: and when he is old, he will not depart from it* (Proverbs 22:6)." The point of this verse is that the training a child receives will always remain with the child. Whether they obey it or not is another issue! Some have erroneously looked at this verse as a guarantee that a child will do right. That is a wrong understanding of what the verse is teaching. We all hope that proper teaching and training leads to perfect obedience; however, the free will of man and his inclination toward sin shatter this idealistic vision.

A parent that has trained the child properly can rest on the fact that the child, wayward or not, knows the right ways of God. Although they might grieve or rejoice about the behavior of their adult children, they should understand and embrace the truth that the adult child is accountable to God for their actions. Training the child was the parent's role. How the child "turns out" is not the litmus test of the truth of the principle. The principle IS true!

The devil also loves to confuse parents with this issue, so the parents throw up their hands and quit, justifying their actions by believing the lie that "the principle does not work all the time." Parents often look at themselves as failures as their adult children wander far from God. The parents can control the teaching and training they give the child, but, as an adult, the will of the child or their child's walk with God is not controlled by the parents.

The parents can control the teaching and training they give the child, but, as an adult, the will of the child or their child's walk with God is not controlled by the parents.

Children are to obey their parents (Ephesians 6:1). They are also to "honor" them, or, as we previously mentioned, consider them precious. These commands come with a promise: "*That it may be well with thee, and that thou mayest live long upon the earth* (Ephesians 6:2)." It is vital for a parent to consistently hold their children accountable for their response to commands and to help them to understand that this is so by the authority of God.

When you take time to think about this, the parenting work is preparatory to the

Parenting work is preparatory to the child's future relationship with God.

45

child's future relationship with God. You want them to honor and obey God too. That is the goal, the parent's primary goal! And then, once the children have grown and have established their own family, the parent/child relationship changes.

It might be a healthy exercise to write down the two greatest struggles you have fulfilling your role/responsibility. By naming them, you might be better equipped to own them and to then begin to change.

Questions to Consider

Are there any areas of this section in which your understanding is in conflict with God's Word?

_____

_____

_____

Has any portion of this section revealed your unhappiness or rebellion about who you are or what your role is?

_____

_____

_____

Has any portion of this section caused you to admit that you have been listening to the

wrong voices and you know it has influenced your thinking in a negative way?

_____

_____

_____

Has this section revealed any flaws in how you have

conducted your marriage relationship?

_____

_____

_____

Chapter 5

Reconciliation: The Basis For Restoration

As much as you may be hurting at the moment, do not lose sight of the great investment you have made in your marriage. If there is any possibility of saving it, you should at least consider the prospect of reconciliation.

The good news is, that God has provided a process for a broken relationship to be repaired. While your pain may be raw at this time, and your emotions ruling the day, a brief time of separation may be helpful. It could serve as a cooling off, or calming down period. This time may allow you an opportunity to give some rational thought to where you have been and where you are headed. While our feelings are real, we must let the truth of God's will be the basis for our actions. God knows what you have been through, and He knows how you feel. God has provided a way for a marriage relationship to formally end if there is no hope of it moving forward. Remember, His original intent was for this marriage to be perfect, and to last for a lifetime, but then sin entered into the equation. In his infinite understanding of mankind, He provided mercy and grace.

A Separation Is Not a Time to Seek a New Relationship

When a marriage is in serious trouble it may be necessary for the couple to separate. God has a purpose in the husband and wife separating for a short time, but it comes with a warning: *"Defraud ye not one the other, except it be with consent for a time, that ye may give yourselves to fasting and prayer; and come together again, that Satan tempt you not for your incontinency* (1 Corinthians 7:5)." They are supposed to fast and pray, focusing, or perhaps re-focusing, on God's intention for their marriage. This is a fragile time as the devil would seek to use the lust of the flesh to challenge their intimacy and gain a dangerous foothold in the life of the couple, destroying their opportunity for reconciliation.

Today, far too many view separation as an acceptable and permanent step, avoiding divorce, because they say, "God hates divorce." That thinking is certainly not in line with the Bible's instruction. Separation is identified in many places in Scripture as "putting away." Consider the following passage from Malachi as he prophesies against the treachery of Judah in her relationship with God:

[13]And this have ye done again, covering the altar of the LORD with tears, with weeping, and with crying out, insomuch that he regardeth not the offering any more, or receiveth it with good will at your hand. [14]Yet ye say, Wherefore? Because the LORD hath been witness between thee and the wife of thy youth, against whom thou hast dealt treacherously: yet is she thy companion, and the wife of thy covenant. [15]And did not he make one? Yet had he the residue of the spirit. And wherefore one? That he might seek a godly seed. Therefore take heed to your spirit, and let none deal treacherously against the wife of his youth. [16]For the LORD, the God of Israel, saith that he hateth putting

away: for one covereth violence with his garment, saith the LORD of hosts: therefore take heed to your spirit, that ye deal not treacherously. [17]Ye have wearied the LORD with your words. Yet ye say, Wherein have we wearied him? When ye say, Every one that doeth evil is good in the sight of the LORD, and he delighteth in them; or, Where is the God of judgment? Malachi 2:13-17

God hates "putting away." The putting away is the real issue, the treacherous treatment by a husband to his wife is what God hates because it violates the principles of marriage and has broken the covenant of the marriage vows. The relationship was damaged, perhaps beyond repair. It was the hardness of the man's heart that allowed it to happen.

The bill of divorcement puts an end to the relationship and finalizes the issue of putting away. It was necessary and provided for in the law of Moses. Yes, it was because of the hardness of the heart, however, it was the remedy to protect the individual and provide them an opportunity to restore their relationship with God. And let me remind you at this point: it does not change the foundation principle "It is not good for a man to be alone."

> *The Bill of Divorcement was the remedy to protect the individual and provide them an opportunity to restore their relationship with God.*

In my study, it also seems to me that a marriage is established when two people commit themselves to each other under the authority of God and they exchange vows to each other. For many different reasons, because we all have a fallen nature, issues arise that strain and then destroy the marriage relationship, resulting in broken vows. Being together, staying together, or living together becomes undesirable/unbearable, even unhealthy—physically, emotionally, and spiritually. While there is fault that may be assigned to both parties, it is often the actions of one of the partners that destroys any opportunity for reconciliation. They separate. However, in separation they are still considered married. If either have a physical relationship with another, they would be committing adultery, and, according to the law, they would be put to death (Leviticus 20:10). The Law no doubt addressed behaviors that were common in the pre-Law period in the culture of the heathen Egyptians. Moses may have been addressing some of these common behaviors when he gave the Law.

> [1] When a man hath taken a wife, and married her, and it come to pass that she find no favour in his eyes, because he hath found some uncleanness in her: then let him write her a bill of divorcement, and give it in her hand, and send her out of his house. [2] And when she is departed out of his house, she may go and be another man's wife. [3] And if the latter husband hate her, and write her a bill of divorcement, and giveth it in her hand, and sendeth her out of his house; or if the latter husband die, which took her to be his wife; *[Mine—in either case the formal marriage had been formally ended]*, [4] her former husband, which sent her away, may not take her again to be his wife, after that she is defiled *[mine—she was sexually active with her other husband]*, for that is abomination before the LORD: and thou shalt not cause the land to sin, which the LORD thy God giveth thee for an inheritance. Deuteronomy 24:1-4

As sinners living in a sinful world, the hardness of men's hearts can cause some difficult circumstances for mankind, and the issue of a troubled marriage is certainly one of those circumstances. The issues of separation, divorce, and remarriage are difficult to be sure. The hypothetical circumstances and the emotional time bombs make it quite complicated.

We do know for sure that "it is not good that man should be alone," and that it was God who brought the woman to Adam to complete him. God's position on this has not changed.

As you well know, mankind, as sinners, has thrown the proverbial monkey wrench into the mix. I suggest you think hard and pray for wisdom and direction on all these issues before ending a marriage.

Getting and Granting Forgiveness

The purpose of forgiveness is to provide a basis on which a relationship can be restored and move forward, leaving the unhealthy past behind. Not so that one would forget the past, but rather that the past failure would not become a permanent barrier to a healthy future. Forgiving and forgetting is a myth, so you may want to adjust your expectations if you have previously bought into that thinking.

We could look at forgiveness as two sides of the same coin. On one side we find "getting" forgiveness. On the other side there is "granting" forgiveness. Speaking proverbially, it takes two to tango; and so, it will take two to reconcile. Whether one is the offender or the offended, there is a biblical responsibility to seek reconciliation. God wants damaged relationships to be restored if at all possible. Jesus taught his disciples this truth in His first teaching session, the Sermon on the Mount (Matthew 5:21-24).

The purpose of forgiveness is to provide a basis on which a relationship can be restored and move forward, leaving the unhealthy past behind.

When facing the issue of reconciliation, it is important to have a clear understanding of the issue(s) of offense. There should be an articulation of the offense(s) so that both sides are clear about what is at the heart of the problem. Each person should listen carefully and respectfully to the other person's side of the story without responding. Let each person speak their piece. "Holding your tongue" and avoiding emotional outbursts projects both respect for the other, and a willingness to engage in this process.

Once you have both aired your grievances, it will likely become obvious what the problem or disagreement is. You should come to an agreement by naming the issue. Then, each person must take responsibility for their part in the offense. Each one should consider confession of their offense and validation of the other person's concern. Both a confession and validation project understanding and agreement. Do not discount the possibility that multiple transgressions may have occurred that have brought you to this point in time. It may be that both have been offenders, and both have been offended.

Next, each party must face the prospect of making a commitment in the process to restore the relationship. The key at this juncture is repentance.

The offender should recognize their fault and ask for forgiveness. They should apologize for committing the offense, and then ask the offended one to forgive them. By seeking forgiveness, they are indicating a willingness both to commit to changing the offending behavior, and to commit to making sure the offense does not happen again. Although the offense may happen again, their intent to change is sincere in their apology.

The offended should then grant forgiveness. They have the choice of granting forgiveness or not, however, the right thing to do is to forgive. This "granting" is a commitment the offended is making that they will never bring up this issue to the offender. They will not "hold it against them." If the grantor of forgiveness does bring up the issue later, they are undermining their own integrity by breaking the commitment they made.

Once these commitments have been made, there is a renewed opportunity for the relationship to move forward. Because of the wounds and scars, the relationship may not be what it was at one time, but the two are now at a place where they can move forward at some peaceable level, leaving the past behind them. It will take both of them doing the right thing—and time—to fully restore trust and integrity, so some patience will be required.

Questions to Consider

Are you willing to try to reconcile? If not, why not?

_____

_____

_____

If God could forgive you, can you forgive another?

_____

_____

_____

Will your decision project an accurate opinion of who God is? Will it glorify Him?

_____

_____

_____

Chapter 6

Rebuilding Your Marriage

O nce reconciled, you have a clean slate upon which you can move forward. *Keep your focus where it belongs; on your responsibility, not theirs!*

Fulfill Your Responsibilities

Remember what your God-given responsibilities are! Focus on fulfilling them. By the grace of God, you have the power to do this! You have also been reminded what your spouse's responsibilities are. Let them focus on doing theirs, and do not discourage or undermine them as they seek to fulfill them.

Draw encouragement from your progress in changing. Do not look to their progress, or rate of change, for encouragement. Be what you can be, do what you can do, and do not let what is out of your control determine your state of mind.

Do not become an enabler of failure! When someone is struggling, or they are not living up to your expectation, jumping in and taking over their responsibility does not fix anything! It only delays the fix, and doing this may cause additional damage. Encourage them to do their part, but let them do their part, even though it falls short of your standard of performance.

Exercise patience as you see them making a good-faith effort. Let them grow! It would serve you well to remember "my way or the highway" is not God's way! Like you, they are the piece of clay on God's pottery wheel that is being shaped into something God wants.

Remember that a question stirs the conscience, but an accusation hardens the will.

A practical suggestion here is this principle: remember that a question stirs the conscience, but an accusation hardens the will. Consider your approach if you are trying to help one see the error of his way. Extending grace and kindness will go a long way toward success in your rebuilding process.

Manage Your Relationships

Take some time right now to name your relationships in priority order and see if it matches the following:

1. **Walking with God—this is the primary relationship, our faith**

2. **Family—our kinfolk or blood relations (first institution God created)**

   a. **Spousal**

   b. **Parent/Child**

   c. **Other family members—including the in-laws and the out-laws!**

3. **Human Government—civic, community relationships (second institution God created)**

   a. **Citizen**

   b. **Neighbor**

4. **Church—our body of Christ relationships (third institution God created)**

   a. **Pastoral**

   b. **Brothers and sisters in Christ**

If you need to make some adjustment to your relationship priorities, do it, and do it now! Managing your relationships going forward means you are constantly evaluating your responsibilities within the role you occupy in each relationship. You can understand the roles of others, but you can only control what you do with yourself. Do yours, not theirs!

> *Managing your relationships going forward means you are constantly evaluating your responsibilities within the role you occupy in each relationship.*

Managing all of these relationships at the same time will provide a balance in your life. You have roles to play and responsibilities to fulfill in each of these institutions.

Questions to Consider

Am I maintaining priority and balance in the relationships I have?

_____

_____

_____

Are there some relationships that need adjusting?

_____

_____

_____

How will I make the adjustments?

_____

_____

_____

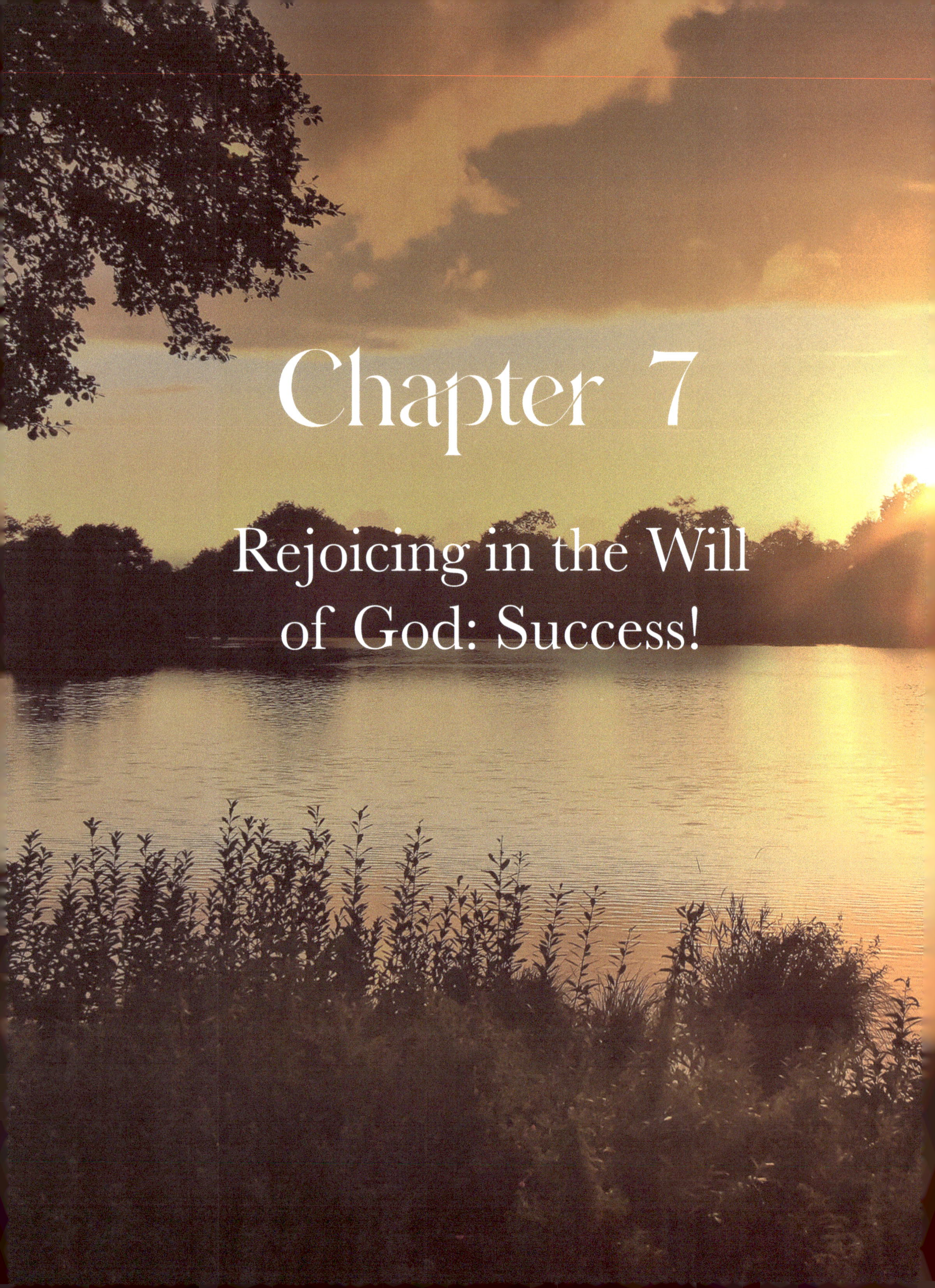

Chapter 7

Rejoicing in the Will of God: Success!

Joy and peace are the fruit of both knowing and doing the will of God. It is the fruit of the Holy Spirit when He is not quenched or grieved by something in our life. These conditions cannot be artificially created; you can only experience them when you trust and obey the Lord.

An honest and open evaluation of your marriage using this framework will be like connecting dots like we did as children in a dot-to-dot book. When the chaos of "dots" is connected with the lines of "truth," a beautiful picture may appear.

Always keep in mind that our lives are about relationships and responsibilities. God's Word provides instruction and counsel so that we can manage relationships and fulfill responsibilities. All we need to know to successfully accomplish this, and live that abundant life that God wants us to enjoy, is found in the Scriptures. The Bible is where you can find the will of God for your life.

God also provides guidance and encouragement through relationships with pastors, teachers (Ephesians 4), and godly friends. Godly counsel is the key. You may find it in other relationships in which you have confidence that their counsel will be with Truth, not personal preference, or opinion.

Be careful not to simply seek someone who will agree with whatever positions you are holding during a difficult time. That is recruiting an army to help you resist or fight, and it will hinder your effort to restore your relationship. A true friend will speak the truth in love. "*Faithful are the wounds of a friend; but the kisses of an enemy are deceitful* (Proverbs 27:6)."

If you can keep this big picture in mind, it will help you in your study of the Scriptures to put what you learn into the proper context. It will bring meaning, understanding, and spiritual depth to your life—living that "abundant life" Jesus spoke of in John 10:10. The Psalmist declared it like this.

> [1] I will extol thee, O LORD; for thou hast lifted me up, and hast not made my foes to rejoice over me. [2] O LORD my God, I cried unto thee, and thou hast healed me. [3] O LORD, thou hast brought up my soul from the grave: thou hast kept me alive, that I should not go down to the pit. [4] Sing unto the LORD, O ye saints of his, and give thanks at the remembrance of his holiness. [5] For his anger endureth but a moment; in his favour is life: weeping may endure for a night, but joy cometh in the morning. Psalm 30:1-5

It's not too late! You have already made significant investments in your marriage. While there may have been difficult and destructive times, there have likely been wonderful and joyous times too. May God bless your honest effort to know what your pathway is moving forward in your life.

It's not too late!

About the Author

Dr. Mike Duffy and his wife of fifty-six years have three children together, twelve grandchildren, and four great-grandchildren. Mike's life experience is characterized by service, integrity, leadership, and accomplishment. He grew up in a home that was shattered by alcoholism when he was in elementary school. Overcoming this tragedy and trauma early in life, he has experienced productivity and success on many levels.

Mike is a combat veteran who served a tour in Vietnam with an infantry battalion of the United States Army's Eighty-Second Airborne Division. He learned the value and reward of working hard early and excelled in a corporate career for fourteen years in administrative management and sales, receiving international awards at each level for outstanding achievement and accomplishment.

Mike received Jesus Christ as his personal Savior at age thirty-one and committed his life to Christian ministry at age thirty-five, ministering God's Word in nearly one thousand ministries nationally and internationally.

He has authored other books based on his life experience including, *The Tragedies and Triumphs in an Alcoholic' Family, Grandpa Saw the Light, It's the City, Stupid* and *The Vivid Colors of the Wounds of War*.

The following statement from Mike reveals his heart: "There is trauma and tragedy everywhere. I believe that everyone will face some adversity in life. How one responds to that adversity will shape their future. People can be paralyzed, damaged, or destroyed when adversity comes, or they can use adversity as motivation for positive change. We cannot change the past, but we do not have to live there, either. We must learn from the past, look toward the future, but live today. Although no one can go back and change their beginning, they can begin today to change their ending. This is what hope looks like. I love serving God and others and have found that this approach in life is the pathway to happiness."

Appendix

Genesis 1 & 2

In the beginning God created the heaven and the earth. ^{2}And the earth was without form, and void; and darkness was upon the face of the deep. And the Spirit of God moved upon the face of the waters.

^{3}And God said, Let there be light: and there was light. ^{4}And God saw the light, that it was good: and God divided the light from the darkness. ^{5}And God called the light Day, and the darkness he called Night. And the evening and the morning were the first day.

^{6}And God said, Let there be a firmament in the midst of the waters, and let it divide the waters from the waters. ^{7}And God made the firmament, and divided the waters which were under the firmament from the waters which were above the firmament: and it was so. ^{8}And God called the firmament Heaven. And the evening and the morning were the second day.

^{9}And God said, Let the waters under the heaven be gathered together unto one place, and let the dry land appear: and it was so. ^{10}And God called the dry land Earth; and the gathering together of the waters called the Seas: and God saw that it was good. ^{11}And God said, Let the earth bring forth grass, the herb yielding seed, and the fruit tree yielding fruit after his kind, whose seed is in itself, upon the earth: and it was so. ^{12}And the earth brought forth grass, and herb yielding seed after his kind, and the tree yielding fruit, whose seed was in itself, after his kind: and God saw that it was good. ^{13}And the evening and the morning were the third day.

^{14}And God said, Let there be lights in the firmament of the heaven to divide the day from the night; and let them be for signs, and for seasons, and for days, and years: ^{15}And let them be for lights in the firmament of the heaven to give light upon the earth:

and it was so. ¹⁶And God made two great lights; the greater light to rule the day, and the lesser light to rule the night: he made the stars also. ¹⁷And God set them in the firmament of the heaven to give light upon the earth, ¹⁸And to rule over the day and over the night, and to divide the light from the darkness: and God saw that it was good. ¹⁹And the evening and the morning were the fourth day.

²⁰And God said, Let the waters bring forth abundantly the moving creature that hath life, and fowl that may fly above the earth in the open firmament of heaven. ²¹And God created great whales, and every living creature that moveth, which the waters brought forth abundantly, after their kind, and every winged fowl after his kind: and God saw that it was good. ²²And God blessed them, saying, Be fruitful, and multiply, and fill the waters in the seas, and let fowl multiply in the earth. ²³And the evening and the morning were the fifth day.

²⁴And God said, Let the earth bring forth the living creature after his kind, cattle, and creeping thing, and beast of the earth after his kind: and it was so. ²⁵And God made the beast of the earth after his kind, and cattle after their kind, and every thing that creepeth upon the earth after his kind: and God saw that it was good.

²⁶And God said, Let us make man in our image, after our likeness: and let them have dominion over the fish of the sea, and over the fowl of the air, and over the cattle, and over all the earth, and over every creeping thing that creepeth upon the earth. ²⁷So God created man in his own image, in the image of God created he him; male and female created he them. ²⁸And God blessed them, and God said unto them, Be fruitful, and multiply, and replenish the earth, and subdue it: and have dominion over the fish of the sea, and over the fowl of the air, and over every living thing that moveth upon the earth. ²⁹And God said, Behold, I have given you every herb bearing seed, which is upon the face of all the earth, and every tree, in the

which is the fruit of a tree yielding seed; to you it shall be for meat. [30]And to every beast of the earth, and to every fowl of the air, and to every thing that creepeth upon the earth, wherein there is life, I have given every green herb for meat: and it was so. [31]And God saw every thing that he had made, and, behold, it was very good. And the evening and the morning were the sixth day.

Genesis 2

Thus the heavens and the earth were finished, and all the host of them. [2]And on the seventh day God ended his work which he had made; and he rested on the seventh day from all his work which he had made. [3]And God blessed the seventh day, and sanctified it: because that in it he had rested from all his work which God created and made.

[4]These are the generations of the heavens and of the earth when they were created, in the day that the LORD God made the earth and the heavens, [5]And every plant of the field before it was in the earth, and every herb of the field before it grew: for the LORD God had not caused it to rain upon the earth, and there was not a man to till the ground. [6]But there went up a mist from the earth, and watered the whole face of the ground. [7]And the LORD God formed man of the dust of the ground, and breathed into his nostrils the breath of life; and man became a living soul.

[8]And the LORD God planted a garden eastward in Eden; and there he put the man whom he had formed. [9]And out of the ground made the LORD God to grow every tree that is pleasant to the sight, and good for food; the tree of life also in the midst of the garden, and the tree of knowledge of good and evil.

[10]And a river went out of Eden to water the garden; and from thence it was parted, and became into four heads. [11]The name of the first is Pison: that is it which compasseth the whole land of Havilah, where there is gold; [12]And the gold of that land is good: there is bdellium and the onyx stone. [13]And the name of the second river is Gihon: the same is it that compasseth the whole land of Ethiopia. [14]And the name of the third river is Hiddekel: that is it which goeth toward the east of Assyria. And the fourth river is Euphrates.

[15]And the LORD God took the man, and put him into the garden of Eden to dress it and to keep it. [16]And the LORD God commanded the man, saying, Of every tree of the garden thou mayest freely eat: [17]But of the tree of the knowledge of good and evil, thou shalt not eat of it: for in the day that thou eatest thereof thou shalt surely die.

[18]And the LORD God said, It is not good that the man should be alone; I will make him an help meet for him. [19]And out of the ground the LORD God formed every beast of the field, and every fowl of the air; and brought them unto Adam to see what he would call them: and whatsoever Adam called every living creature, that was the name thereof. [20]And Adam gave names to all cattle, and to the fowl of the air, and to every beast of the field; but for Adam there was not found an help meet for him.

[21]And the LORD God caused a deep sleep to fall upon Adam, and he slept: and he took one of his ribs, and closed up the flesh instead thereof; [22]And the rib, which the LORD God had taken from man, made he a woman, and brought her unto the man.

[23]And Adam said, This is now bone of my bones, and flesh of my flesh: she shall be called Woman, because she was taken out of Man.

[24]Therefore shall a man leave his father and his mother, and shall cleave unto his wife: and they shall be one flesh. [25]And they were both naked, the man and his wife, and were not ashamed.

Ephesians 4

I therefore, the prisoner of the Lord, beseech you that ye walk worthy of the vocation wherewith ye are called, [2]With all lowliness and meekness, with longsuffering, forbearing one another in love; [3]Endeavouring to keep the unity of the Spirit in the bond of peace. [4]There is one body, and one Spirit, even as ye are called in one hope of your calling; [5]One Lord, one faith, one baptism, [6]One God and Father of all, who is above all, and through all, and in you all.

[7]But unto every one of us is given grace according to the measure of the gift of Christ.

[8]Wherefore he saith, When he ascended up on high, he led captivity captive, and gave gifts unto men.

[9](Now that he ascended, what is it but that he also descended first into the lower parts of the earth? [10]He that descended is the same also that ascended up far above all heavens, that he might fill all things.) [11]And he gave some, apostles; and some, prophets; and some, evangelists; and some, pastors and teachers; [12]For the perfecting of the saints, for the work of the ministry, for the edifying of the body of Christ: [13]Till we all come in the unity of the faith, and of the knowledge of the Son of God, unto a perfect man, unto the measure of the stature of the fulness of Christ: [14]That we henceforth be no more children, tossed to and fro, and carried about with every wind of doctrine, by the sleight of men, and cunning craftiness, whereby they lie in wait to deceive; [15]But speaking the truth in love, may grow up into him in all things, which is the head, even Christ: [16]From whom the whole body fitly joined together and compacted by that which every joint supplieth, according to the effectual working in the measure of every part, maketh increase of the body unto the edifying of itself in love.

[17]This I say therefore, and testify in the Lord, that ye henceforth walk not as other Gentiles walk, in the vanity of their mind, [18]Having the understanding darkened, being alienated from the life of God through the ignorance that is in them, because of the blindness of their heart: [19]Who being past feeling have given themselves over unto lasciviousness, to work all uncleanness with greediness. [20]But ye have not so learned Christ; [21]If so be that ye have heard him, and have been taught by him, as the truth is in Jesus: [22]That ye put off concerning the former conversation the old man, which is corrupt according to the deceitful lusts; [23]And be renewed in the spirit of your mind; [24]And that ye put on the new man, which after God is created in righteousness and true holiness.

[25]Wherefore putting away lying, speak every man truth with his neighbour: for we are members one of another. [26]Be ye angry, and sin not: let not the sun go down upon your wrath: [27]Neither give place to the devil. [28]Let him that stole steal no more: but rather let him labour, working with his hands the thing which is good, that he may have to give to him that needeth. [29]Let no corrupt communication proceed out of your mouth, but that which is good to the use of edifying, that it may minister grace unto the hearers. [30]And grieve not the holy Spirit of God, whereby ye are sealed unto the day of redemption. [31]Let all bitterness, and wrath, and anger, and clamour, and evil speaking, be put away from you, with all malice: [32]And be ye kind one to another, tenderhearted, forgiving one another, even as God for Christ's sake hath forgiven you.

Ephesians 5

Be ye therefore followers of God, as dear children; [2]And walk in love, as Christ also hath loved us, and hath given himself for us an offering and a sacrifice to God for a sweetsmelling savour.

[3]But fornication, and all uncleanness, or covetousness, let it not be once named among you, as becometh saints; [4]Neither filthiness, nor foolish talking, nor jesting, which are not convenient: but rather giving of thanks. [5]For this ye know, that no whoremonger, nor unclean person, nor covetous man, who is an idolater, hath any inheritance in the kingdom of Christ and of God.

[6]Let no man deceive you with vain words: for because of these things cometh the wrath of God upon the children of disobedience. [7]Be not ye therefore partakers with them.

[8]For ye were sometimes darkness, but now are ye light in the Lord: walk as children of light: [9](For the fruit of the Spirit is in all goodness, righteousness, and truth;) [10]Proving what is acceptable unto the Lord. [11]And have no fellowship with the unfruitful works of darkness, but rather reprove them. [12]For it is a shame even to speak of those things which are done of them in secret. [13]But all things that are reproved are made manifest by the light: for whatsoever doth make manifest is light.

[14]Wherefore he saith, Awake thou that sleepest, and arise from the dead, and Christ shall give thee light.

[15]See then that ye walk circumspectly, not as fools, but as wise, [16]Redeeming the time, because the days are evil. [17]Wherefore be ye not unwise, but understanding what the will of the Lord is. [18]And be not drunk with wine, wherein is excess; but be filled with the Spirit; [19]Speaking to yourselves in psalms and hymns and spiritual songs, singing and making melody in your heart to the Lord; [20]Giving thanks

always for all things unto God and the Father in the name of our Lord Jesus Christ; [21]Submitting yourselves one to another in the fear of God.

[22]Wives, submit yourselves unto your own husbands, as unto the Lord. [23]For the husband is the head of the wife, even as Christ is the head of the church: and he is the saviour of the body. [24]Therefore as the church is subject unto Christ, so let the wives be to their own husbands in every thing.

[25]Husbands, love your wives, even as Christ also loved the church, and gave himself for it; [26]That he might sanctify and cleanse it with the washing of water by the word, [27]That he might present it to himself a glorious church, not having spot, or wrinkle, or any such thing; but that it should be holy and without blemish. [28]So ought men to love their wives as their own bodies. He that loveth his wife loveth himself. [29]For no man ever yet hated his own flesh; but nourisheth and cherisheth it, even as the Lord the church: [30]For we are members of his body, of his flesh, and of his bones. [31]For this cause shall a man leave his father and mother, and shall be joined unto his wife, and they two shall be one flesh. [32]This is a great mystery: but I speak concerning Christ and the church. [33]Nevertheless let every one of you in particular so love his wife even as himself; and the wife see that she reverence her husband.

Colossians 3

If ye then be risen with Christ, seek those things which are above, where Christ sitteth on the right hand of God. ² Set your affection on things above, not on things on the earth. ³ For ye are dead, and your life is hid with Christ in God. ⁴ When Christ, who is our life, shall appear, then shall ye also appear with him in glory.

⁵ Mortify therefore your members which are upon the earth; fornication, uncleanness, inordinate affection, evil concupiscence, and covetousness, which is idolatry: ⁶ For which things' sake the wrath of God cometh on the children of disobedience: ⁷ In the which ye also walked some time, when ye lived in them. ⁸ But now ye also put off all these; anger, wrath, malice, blasphemy, filthy communication out of your mouth. ⁹ Lie not one to another, seeing that ye have put off the old man with his deeds; ¹⁰ And have put on the new man, which is renewed in knowledge after the image of him that created him: ¹¹ Where there is neither Greek nor Jew, circumcision nor uncircumcision, Barbarian, Scythian, bond nor free: but Christ is all, and in all.

¹² Put on therefore, as the elect of God, holy and beloved, bowels of mercies, kindness, humbleness of mind, meekness, longsuffering; ¹³ Forbearing one another, and forgiving one another, if any man have a quarrel against any: even as Christ forgave you, so also do ye. ¹⁴ And above all these things put on charity, which is the bond of perfectness. ¹⁵ And let the peace of God rule in your hearts, to the which also ye are called in one body; and be ye thankful. ¹⁶ Let the word of Christ dwell in you richly in all wisdom; teaching and admonishing one another in psalms and hymns and spiritual songs, singing with grace in your hearts to the Lord. ¹⁷ And whatsoever ye do in word or deed, do all in the name of the Lord Jesus, giving thanks to God and the Father by him.

[18] Wives, submit yourselves unto your own husbands, as it is fit in the Lord. [19] Husbands, love your wives, and be not bitter against them. [20] Children, obey your parents in all things: for this is well pleasing unto the Lord. [21] Fathers, provoke not your children to anger, lest they be discouraged.

[22] Servants, obey in all things your masters according to the flesh; not with eyeservice, as menpleasers; but in singleness of heart, fearing God: [23] And whatsoever ye do, do it heartily, as to the Lord, and not unto men; [24] Knowing that of the Lord ye shall receive the reward of the inheritance: for ye serve the Lord Christ. [25] But he that doeth wrong shall receive for the wrong which he hath done: and there is no respect of persons.

Colossians 4

Masters, give unto your servants that which is just and equal; knowing that ye also have a Master in heaven.

[2] Continue in prayer, and watch in the same with thanksgiving; [3] Withal praying also for us, that God would open unto us a door of utterance, to speak the mystery of Christ, for which I am also in bonds: [4] That I may make it manifest, as I ought to speak.

[5] Walk in wisdom toward them that are without, redeeming the time. [6] Let your speech be alway with grace, seasoned with salt, that ye may know how ye ought to answer every man.

[7] All my state shall Tychicus declare unto you, who is a beloved brother, and a faithful minister and fellowservant in the Lord: [8] Whom I have sent unto you for the same purpose, that he might know your estate, and comfort your hearts; [9] With Onesimus, a faithful and beloved brother, who is one of you. They shall make known unto you all things which are done here.

¹⁰ Aristarchus my fellowprisoner saluteth you, and Marcus, sister's son to Barnabas, (touching whom ye received commandments: if he come unto you, receive him;) ¹¹ And Jesus, which is called Justus, who are of the circumcision. These only are my fellowworkers unto the kingdom of God, which have been a comfort unto me. ¹² Epaphras, who is one of you, a servant of Christ, saluteth you, always labouring fervently for you in prayers, that ye may stand perfect and complete in all the will of God. ¹³ For I bear him record, that he hath a great zeal for you, and them that are in Laodicea, and them in Hierapolis. ¹⁴ Luke, the beloved physician, and Demas, greet you. ¹⁵ Salute the brethren which are in Laodicea, and Nymphas, and the church which is in his house.

¹⁶ And when this epistle is read among you, cause that it be read also in the church of the Laodiceans; and that ye likewise read the epistle from Laodicea. ¹⁷ And say to Archippus, Take heed to the ministry which thou hast received in the Lord, that thou fulfil it.

¹⁸ The salutation by the hand of me Paul. Remember my bonds. Grace be with you. Amen.

(Written from Rome to Colossians by Tychicus and Onesimus.)

MORE BOOKS BY DR. MIKE DUFFY

It's the Cities, Stupid!

The Vivid Colors of the Wounds of War

Grandpa Saw the Light

The Tragedies and Triumphs in an Alcoholic's Family

www.ingramcontent.com/pod-product-compliance
Lightning Source LLC
Chambersburg PA
CBHW042347030426

42335CB00031B/3490